World-Class Service

World-Class
Service

101 ways to
deliver exceptional
customer experiences

MONIQUE RICHARDSON

Published by Monique Richardson

First published in 2024 in Melbourne, Australia

Copyright © Monique Richardson

www.moniquerichardson.com.au

The moral rights of the author have been asserted.

Edited by Jenny Magee

Typeset by BookPOD

ISBN: 978-0-6457927-2-0 (pbk) ISBN: 978-0-6457927-3-7 (ebook)

A catalogue record for this book is available from the National Library of Australia

Dedication

⸻ ✺ ⸻

This book is dedicated to my beautiful Mum,
Marea Richardson, for reading every one of my newsletters
and encouraging me to write this book.

'If world-class was easy,

everyone would be doing it.'

Robin Sharma

Contents

Part Two: World-Class Communication Skills

Part Three: Manage Challenging Situations

Part Four: Self-care and Resilience

Preface

I fell in love with customer service at the ripe old age of 14 years and 9 months when I started working part-time at a supermarket. There was something about connecting with people and seeing the impact of service. Whether remembering customers' orders or recognising regulars, I learnt quickly about the power of human connection.

After leaving school, I transitioned into frontline roles in hospitality, retail and contact centres. I cherished every job. Then, by chance, I was asked to design and deliver a training workshop. At that moment, I knew I had found what I wanted to do for the rest of my life. Ending my last full-time role as a national training manager, I combined my two greatest passions of customer service and learning and development. For more than two decades, I have been privileged to work across every industry imaginable, providing workshops and keynotes to over 50,000 people.

I have enormous love, respect and care for our customer service community. I am passionate about ensuring they are cared for, protected and valued, as I know all too well the mindset and dedication required to show up and deliver world-class service every day. Recent years have been even more challenging, with lockdowns, stock and labour shortages, and increasingly difficult and aggressive customer behaviour.

I began my weekly email newsletter in 2020. To this day, I still love hearing from my community how much that information has helped or resonated. This book was inspired by the tips and ideas I shared in the newsletter. Each tip has an accompanying quote. I have collected quotes for as long as I can remember and find them a constant source of inspiration.

These tips encompass various aspects of delivering world-class service, from mindset and communication to managing challenging situations and resilience. Incorporating these practices into your daily interactions will support you to create exceptional customer experiences and contribute to a culture of service excellence within your organisation.

You can use this book in many ways:

- Open a random page
- Choose a focus for your day
- Choose a focus for your week
- Choose a focus for the daily or weekly team huddle
- Read the entire book from front to back.

World-class service is not a destination; it's a mindset, a way of being and a personal commitment to be the best of the best. It is not defined by luxury or five-star ratings but by the desire to deliver a world-class experience regardless of the industry or task. It's a continuous journey of growth and improvement, the never-ending pursuit of excellence.

By embodying these principles, you can create a lasting legacy of exceptional service.

The power of customer experience, empathy and kindness knows no bounds. Every day, we have an opportunity to create impactful connections and leave lasting impressions. I am so proud to be part of such an incredible community of people who make a difference in the lives of others every day.

Yours in service,

Monique (she/her)

'Everybody can be great ... because anybody can serve. You don't need a college degree to serve. You don't have to make your subject and verb agree to serve. You only need a heart full of grace. A soul generated by love.'

MARTIN LUTHER KING JR

Part One

World-Class
Service Delivery

'Act as if what you do makes
a difference. It does.'

WILLIAM JAMES

Believe you make a difference

You are important. Every day, when you arrive at work, take a moment to consider the significance of your work. Reflect on how it contributes to the overall customer experience and the impact on those you serve.

Purpose, consciously embraced, is powerful. Make it a focal point at the beginning of each day, and watch your perspective transform. Your work will no longer be just a task or a process. Each day will be an opportunity to brighten someone's day, enhance their experience, or even change their life.

Your actions have the potential to create ripples that extend far beyond the confines of your workplace.

Every interaction is an opportunity to make a positive difference in someone's life. Embrace this responsibility with intention and compassion.

*'Our greatest freedom is the
freedom to choose our attitude.'*

Viktor E. Frankl

Choose your attitude

World-class customer service begins with a conscious choice. You get to choose your attitude. At the start of every day, set an intention for how you want to show up and how you will be of service.

Attitude makes a significant difference to a customer's experience. Approach every interaction with enthusiasm and a smile. Some days will be more challenging than others and you may need to dig deeper on those days.

Remember that your attitude affects the customer and influences the overall perception of your organisation. Choose a mindset that radiates warmth, positivity and a genuine willingness to go the extra mile. Make every customer interaction a world-class experience.

'The friendly smile, the word of greeting, are certainly something fleeting and seemingly insubstantial. You can't take them with you. But they work for good beyond your power to measure their influence. It is the service we are not obliged to give that people value most.'

JAMES CASH PENNEY

Greet with intent

~∽⌒~

Your initial greeting builds rapport with your customer.

Whether in person, over the phone or through digital communication, be focused, friendly and ready to help the customer with a positive and welcoming attitude.

Offer a warm smile and use their name if available. Begin with a polite and friendly greeting, such as 'Good morning, [Customer's name]! How can I assist you today?' or 'Welcome!'.

A warm and friendly greeting is the foundation of all positive customer interactions.

'We are what we repeatedly do. Excellence,
therefore, is not an act, but a habit.'

ARISTOTLE

Set high personal standards

Establish uncompromising personal standards for service quality. That means demanding excellence of yourself in everything you do. It involves a commitment to integrity, accountability and continuous improvement.

Be relentless in your pursuit of excellence.

Deliver consistently on your promises.

Honour your word and your commitments.

Hold yourself accountable for the standards you set, but be gentle with yourself if you fail to meet them. Identify what happened and why, then take measures to ensure it doesn't happen again.

A mindset of excellence makes a significant difference to everything you do.

'It is better to anticipate than to react.'

BOBBY KNIGHT

Anticipate customer needs

Pay close attention to what your customers say – and what they don't say. Their tone and body language can offer insights into their unspoken needs.

If you sense a customer needs your help, reach out first. Seek opportunities to address any potential issues or enquiries, whether you're connecting face-to-face or online.

Look for the next problem to solve or question to answer. Listen and respond to the customer's expressed and unexpressed needs.

'I've learned that people will forget
what you said, people will forget
what you did, but people will never
forget how you made them feel.'

MAYA ANGELOU

Create positive emotions

How you make customers feel impacts their decision to return.

Always ask yourself, 'How do I want my customer to feel?' Focus on creating interactions that evoke positive emotional responses.

The experience you create directly influences the customer's emotional state. Positive experiences foster positive emotions. Negative experiences generate negative emotions. Customers who receive world-class service feel happy, grateful, impressed and valued. Poor service leaves them disappointed, let down, upset and even angry.

What has the greatest impact on customer emotions? It's the people who serve them.

Make sure your customers feel cared for, heard and understood.

'It's the little things that make the big things possible. Only close attention to the fine details of any operation makes the operation first class.'

J. WILLARD MARRIOTT

Mind the details

Paying attention to detail is more than a practice; it is a way of being. It involves every element of the service experience, from design to delivery.

Every interaction, no matter how small, holds the potential to enhance or detract from the customer's experience. That starts with the initial greeting and goes to the final farewell. It's remembering how to pronounce a customer's name, confirming the accuracy of any information and ensuring the service environment is clean and welcoming. Every detail contributes to the overall perception of service quality.

Meticulous attention to detail elevates service from good to world-class.

'If you're not serving the customer, your

job is to be serving someone who is.'

JAN CARLZON

All great service starts at home

The foundation of exceptional organisational service cultures is ensuring everyone understands who their customers are and how their role impacts the overall customer experience.

Customer service is everyone's responsibility. Beyond external customers, it's serving internal customers within our organisations. These include our teams, people in other departments, our colleagues and leaders.

All exceptional customer experiences start at home. How we respect and treat each other ultimately flows onto the customer. View internal customers as valued partners. While the relationship may be more informal, being responsive and reliable are equally important.

'Remember that a person's name is, to that person, the sweetest and most important sound in any language.'

DALE CARNEGIE

Use the customer's name

Building personal connections with customers is a valuable opportunity in a world where human touchpoints are diminishing.

The use of names is a simple yet powerful way to connect.

Where appropriate, introduce yourself and ask for their name. Using and remembering names makes customers feel valued and important. If their name is challenging to pronounce, confirm it with them. Ask, 'How should I say your name?'

Make sure you spell names correctly, too. If it helps, make a note to remind you how to pronounce the name correctly.

It's a great way to build rapport. Incorporating this habit into your interactions makes customers feel recognised, seen, cared for and important.

'Because of your smile, you
make life more beautiful.'

THICH NHAT HANH

Smile

In delivering world-class service, the power of a smile cannot be overstated. It's more than a universally recognised symbol of warmth and hospitality. A genuine smile communicates friendliness and approachability, setting the tone for positive engagement.

Whether in person or over the phone, approach every conversation with a smile to create an atmosphere of openness and receptiveness and pave the way for meaningful connections.

The act of smiling benefits everyone. Scientific research reveals that smiling triggers the release of endorphins, the body's natural feel-good hormones, promoting a sense of wellbeing and reducing stress. As a bonus, smiles are contagious, spreading positivity and enhancing the overall experience for customers and service providers.

Incorporating smiles into every interaction is more than a gesture of hospitality; it's a powerful tool for creating exceptional service encounters.

*'Could a greater miracle take place
than for us to look through each
other's eyes for an instant?'*

HENRY DAVID THOREAU

Put yourself in their shoes

Empathy is the foundation of customer service and caring, healthy societies and workplaces. It is the ability to step into another person's shoes, comprehend their feelings and perspectives and use that understanding to guide your actions.

Immersing yourself in the customer's way of thinking offers a fresh lens into their world. Take a moment to pause and truly engage with your customers. What emotions are they experiencing? Delve into understanding their thoughts and feelings and recognise and address their underlying sources of frustrations and pain points.

Empathy is one of the most powerful tools for fostering connection.

'Do more than just talk; act. Do more than just promise; deliver.'

DR STEVE MARABOLI

Do what you say you will

Delivering on your promises demonstrates integrity.

One of the most potent ways to build trust and lasting relationships with customers is by making realistic promises and always following through on your word.

Every. Single. Time.

Your response is critical if something unforeseen happens and you cannot meet a promised deadline. World-class service providers take immediate action instead of avoiding the issue or making excuses. They proactively communicate with the customer as early as possible, acknowledge the situation, and swiftly work to re-establish a new timeframe.

This level of accountability mitigates potential damage to the customer relationship and strengthens trust and confidence in your personal brand. Customers recognise and appreciate honesty and professionalism when challenges arise. Consistently upholding your commitments, solidifies your reputation as a provider of world-class service.

*'We see our customers as invited guests
to a party, and we are the hosts. It's
our job to make every aspect of the
customer experience a little bit better.'*

JEFF BEZOS

Reduce customer effort

Delivering a seamless, easy and effortless experience is essential to providing world-class service.

Customer effort measures the exertion customers must invest in resolving issues, following up on phone calls or emails not responded to, fulfilling requests or obtaining answers. It encompasses four areas: cognitive effort (mental processing), time effort (waiting, consuming, transacting), physical effort (physical energy) and emotional effort (negative vs. positive energy).

Minimise the need for customers to follow up, repeat information or engage in multiple interactions. Make customer ease and convenience a daily priority.

The question 'How can I make my customers' lives easier?' should guide every decision and interaction.

'Always render more and better
service than is expected of you, no
matter what your task may be.'

OG MANDINO

Deliver 'plus one' moments

To create memorable experiences, look for ways to surprise and delight your customers. Use your service to create a genuine emotional connection by remembering names, preferences, important details or previous conversations.

Plan delightful surprises or moments of joy for your customers. Whether it's a spontaneous gesture, a handwritten thank-you note or a personalised gift, these acts of kindness show your appreciation and make them feel valued and special.

Strive to create remarkable experiences, not just good ones. Experiences that leave an enduring positive impression become stories worth sharing. Consistently delivering these 'plus one' moments sets your service apart.

'Make the customer's problem

your problem.'

Shep Hyken

Take ownership

Enhancing the customer experience involves a proactive approach that assumes ownership and accountability for achieving first-contact resolution.

Handballing or transferring customers from one person or department to another is deeply frustrating. In a world-class service environment, saying, 'It's not my responsibility' is simply not an option.

While there may be multiple departments within an organisation, delivering exceptional service requires a united and cohesive team effort.

Go the extra mile. Adopt an unwavering 'whatever it takes' mindset.

If it is genuinely something you cannot assist with, embrace the responsibility of identifying the appropriate department or individual and facilitating direct contact. Your customers will appreciate your efforts.

'Nothing great was ever achieved without enthusiasm.'

Ralph Waldo Emerson

It's always opening night

~~∞~~

Have you ever sat in the audience of a musical, concert, drama or comedy show? If so, you'll know the feeling of excitement and anticipation just before the curtain rises.

For the singer, musician or performer, this could be the tenth, twentieth or seventieth time they have performed the show. Imagine if they were to step onto the stage and deliver it as though it were their fiftieth performance. And now imagine the different energy of opening night.

It's the same working in customer service, where you may interact with multiple customers, take phone calls or be asked the same question for the hundredth time.

Embrace a performer's mindset. Treat each customer as if they are the first person of the day. It will transform their experience.

'The key is to set realistic
customer expectations, then
exceed them – preferably in
unexpected and helpful ways.'

RICHARD BRANSON

Manage customer expectations

Customers deserve to be well-informed; doing so requires setting manageable time frames and realistic expectations. Discuss potential solutions and be specific about what is feasible. Provide clear timelines, explore options and involve them in the resolution process.

Transparency is crucial. Even if the outcome is not what the customer wants, deliver the message honestly and with empathy to avoid future issues and disappointment.

Deliver on your promises. Fulfilling commitments builds customer trust and confidence, so it is critical to managing expectations. Keep customers updated, follow through and inform them when you have delivered.

Remain polite and respectful, but remember it's ok to be assertive when faced with unrealistic demands. Be upfront, honest and understanding.

'Meet first, exceed second.'

KEN BLANCHARD

Focus on the fundamentals

Consistently delivering on the basics is the key to creating raving fans. Before you create 'plus one' moments or exceed expectations, make sure the basics are flawlessly executed.

True excellence is demonstrated by consistency in every interaction. Dedication to getting the fundamentals right is the first step in creating memorable experiences that set your service apart.

'You never get a second chance
to make a first impression.'

Will Rogers

Create powerful first impressions

Customers form first impressions within seconds of encountering a person, product or business.

These impressions are based on everything from human touchpoints to a website, email or live chat.

Visual appearance matters. Customers will notice your surroundings, your clothing, grooming and cleanliness.

Your posture, facial expressions and gestures convey your attitude and demeanour.

How you speak – your telephone manner, tone of voice, clarity and choice of words create an impression of friendliness, while inattention or rudeness can have the opposite effect.

Remember, behaviour breeds behaviour and first impressions last, so make a positive impact.

'Start going the extra mile and
opportunity will follow you.'

Napoleon Hill

Guide customers where they need to go

Have you ever asked for directions only to receive complicated or inaccurate information that left you feeling lost and frustrated?

While it may seem a minor detail, a powerful way to enhance the customer experience is by responding with a friendly and helpful, 'Let me show you.'

That is far better than 'Would you like me to show you?'. Customers may not want to inconvenience you, even if they need your help!

When you take the extra step to personally guide a customer to their desired destination or item, you smooth their journey, provide an opportunity for conversation along the way and build rapport.

This simple gesture can leave a lasting positive impression and create a memorable customer experience.

'Everyone has an invisible sign hanging
from their neck saying, "Make me
feel important". Never forget this
message when working with people.'

Mary Kay Ash

Implement the 10-5-3 rule

Widely used in the hospitality industry, five-star hotels and retail businesses, the 10-5-3 rule outlines specific actions for interacting with customers based on proximity.

Within 10 feet, acknowledge the customer with a genuine smile or eye contact to convey a sense of attentiveness and appreciation, even before they've sought assistance. This initial encounter sets the tone for the entire interaction.

As the customer draws nearer, within 5 feet, greet them warmly with a verbal acknowledgement, such as 'Hello' or a time-of-the-day salutation, such as 'Good morning.' This personal touch extends a warm welcome and is the first step in building rapport.

Within 3 feet, anticipate the customer's needs, offer assistance or enquire if they require specific help. Opt for an open-ended question such as 'How can I help you?' to demonstrate a genuine desire to understand and address their needs.

Personalised attention creates a friendly and welcoming environment. These simple yet powerful gestures make your customers feel noticed and valued.

'Multi-tasking is a persistent myth.
Paying deep, focused attention to one
task at a time is the correct way.'

CAROLINE LEAF

Focus your attention

Customer service often requires handling multiple tasks simultaneously, but it's best to avoid multi-tasking wherever possible.

Dividing your attention increases the chances of errors and inaccuracy, leading to complaints and dissatisfied customers. It limits your ability to build rapport and connection.

So, focus on one task at a time.

Giving each customer your undivided attention means you can resolve their enquiries efficiently. Once a task is completed satisfactorily, move on to the next, ensuring a seamless and productive workflow.

Attentive and focused customer service is about creating positive experiences and getting things right the first time.

'Eat a live frog first thing in the morning, and nothing worse will happen to you for the rest of the day.'

MARK TWAIN

Schedule first things first

Prioritise your essential objectives amid the regular, daily tasks that compete for your attention.

Embrace challenging tasks such as making important calls or engaging in difficult conversations first.

Identify your peak productivity hours to tackle the most critical tasks effectively. Enhance your focus and effectiveness by aligning your work with your most productive times.

'Between stimulus and response, there is a space. In that space is our power to choose our response. In our response lies our growth and our freedom.'

VIKTOR E. FRANKL

Deliver exceptional service – even on challenging days

We all have lives outside of work, which are sometimes complex and challenging.

You may be supporting an elderly or unwell parent. Maybe you lay awake all night grieving a relationship breakup. Perhaps you are dealing with uncooperative children. You feel unwell. Or you got stuck in traffic on the way to work this morning.

It's not always easy to turn up to work with a positive mindset. You are human. You have feelings and emotions, and some things in life are bigger than work. Reaching out to a trusted leader or colleague can make all the difference at these times.

While many things can affect your mood, it is not ok to use 'I'm just having a bad day' as an excuse for poor customer service delivery.

You can't always control what happens, but you can always choose how you respond.

There is never any excuse to be rude to a customer or co-worker. Find a way to remain present and positive, as it directly impacts your customers' and colleagues' experience.

Ask yourself, 'Would I like to be served by me today?'

'Our lives begin to end the day we
become silent about things that matter.'

MARTIN LUTHER KING

Speak up and share your ideas

The most valuable insights on improving customer experience come from two main sources: your customers and those who work directly with them.

Given that you are in regular contact with customers, you have a unique perspective for ideas and initiatives to enhance their experience. Through your conversations with them, you gather firsthand knowledge of customer pain points, frustrations and obstacles. You'll hear phrases like 'It would be easier if ...' or 'It is really difficult when ...'.

Some of the most effective improvements originate on the frontline, so share customer feedback and ideas with your team and leaders.

Your voice matters in shaping exceptional customer experiences.

'*Let us be grateful to the people who*
make us happy; they are the charming
gardeners who make our souls blossom.'

MARCEL PROUST

Be grateful more often

Express gratitude to your external and internal customers.

Focus on thoughtful and inexpensive acts that show you care.

Send a heartfelt handwritten note or card to express your appreciation.

Arrange a morning tea to foster internal connection.

Close the feedback loop by sharing how customer input has enhanced the experience.

Personally contact customers. Pick up the phone and see how things are going rather than sending an email.

Recognise and acknowledge loyal customers, referrers and long-term customers.

Who could you thank today?

'*When everyone is included, everyone wins.*'

JESSE JACKSON

Foster inclusive customer service

Accessibility is a cornerstone of genuine customer-centricity, reflecting a commitment to inclusivity, respect and personalised care. Every customer should feel welcomed, valued and fully supported in accessing the services they require.

People facing accessibility barriers should never be an afterthought or compelled to settle for a lesser experience in terms of service, quality, convenience or communication.

Inclusive customer service means prioritising individuals and preserving their dignity. Consider religious and cultural beliefs and learn what it takes to meet customer needs.

Avoid making assumptions about needs or capabilities; instead, respectfully enquire how you can best assist them while honouring their preferences and autonomy.

Always address the person directly, not their caregiver, support person or interpreter.

Actively and attentively listen to their needs, utilising appropriate body language and maintaining eye contact. Never touch a customer without their explicit permission.

Lastly, don't assume someone needs your help; instead, offer assistance respectfully and wait for their response.

'To me, the future is personalization.'

Marissa Mayer

Make personalisation meaningful

Personalisation is essential in creating world-class experiences. It shows deep care and consideration, so learn what matters to them.

Keep detailed records of customer preferences. Note any comments in bookings or customer notes and act accordingly. Include the correct pronunciation of their name. Celebrate milestones and anniversaries with personalised messages and thoughtful gifts or gestures you know they will appreciate.

Be clear on how, when and if they prefer you to contact them.

For surprise and delight moments, learn about them. Are they gluten-free? Do they eat chocolate? Do they prefer bubbles, red or white wine or no alcohol? What are their interests and hobbies?

One size doesn't fit all.

Tell your customers they matter to you by customising your service to accommodate individual preferences, needs and special requests.

'Speed, agility and responsiveness
are the keys to future success.'

ANITA RODDICK

Be highly responsive

Customer expectations around response times are rising with increases in automation, AI, technology and self-service.

Customers equate responsiveness with care.

If you don't have an immediate answer, acknowledge the email, phone call or message. That will reduce the customer's stress. Even an auto-acknowledgement provides reassurance that their message has been received.

Confirm when you will get back to them and honour that commitment.

Provide regular progress reports and updates by leveraging technology such as SMS updates or email. If there are unforeseen delays, update the customer well before the deadline.

'First impressions are important, but the last impression we leave with the customer will leave the most lasting impression.'

SHEP HYKEN

Deliver a fond farewell

One of the final elements of the customer journey is farewelling them or closing the interaction.

Conclude every conversation on a friendly, courteous note. Leave the customer with a smile, reassuring them that their concerns are heard and acted on.

Thank them for their time or patronage.

Do a final check-in by asking, 'Is there anything further I can assist you with today?' or 'Do you have any final questions?'

Giving them a moment to consider may avoid unnecessary future contact.

Personalise your farewell with meaningful information gleaned in your conversation, such as, 'Have a wonderful trip away this weekend'.

By consistently delivering world-class service right up to the last minute, you strengthen customer loyalty and leave a positive impression that resonates long after the conversation ends.

'Education is the most powerful weapon
which you can use to change the world.'

Nelson Mandela

Educate and inform

Customers have varying levels of knowledge, so inform, educate and empower them whenever possible.

Whether you provide detailed explanations of a process, send informative materials or guide them through self-service options, your goal is to equip customers with the knowledge and confidence they need.

Never say, 'It's on the website'. Show them. Send a link. Assist customers in the present and prepare them for future interactions.

'Don't worry about what you can't control. Our focus and energy need to be on the things we can control. Attitude, effort, focus – these are the things we can control.'

TIM TEBOW

Control the controllable

In customer service, some things are always within your control (your attitude and mindset), while others are outside your control (customer mood or attitude, systems, processes and technology).

Positive, proactive people focus on what they can control, influence or change. They recognise the challenges associated with elements beyond their control and choose not to focus on them. Instead, they suggest improvements and leave the outcome to unfold.

You have limited energy for the day, so choose where and how best to expend it.

When you feel negative, ask yourself, 'Is this something I can control, influence or change?'

If it is, take immediate action.

If not, acknowledge the challenges, then choose not to stay stuck. Move forward.

'If you are 15 minutes early, you are on time. If you are on time, you are late, and if you are late, you didn't want to be there.'

VINCE LOMBARDI

Be punctual

—✎—

Punctuality is more than just meeting deadlines; it's a tangible display of your dedication to providing outstanding service. Being on time for appointments, in-person or virtual meetings, or service delivery demonstrates commitment and respect. It shows that you value your customer's time.

Anticipate potential delays and build buffers into your schedule. Aim to arrive a few minutes early whenever possible.

Being on time for a shift or logged in ready to take calls leads to better time management and workflow efficiency. That ultimately benefits the customer through faster service or responses.

'Accuracy builds credibility.'

JIM ROHN

Get things right the first time

To avoid complaints and rework and save time and resources, focus on getting things right the first time.

That means simple actions like spelling customer names accurately and ensuring you have their correct address.

Attention to detail takes conscious effort, so make it a fundamental requirement of all aspects of your work.

It will benefit both you and your customers.

'*Everyone has a personal brand,*
by design or by default.'

LIDA CITROEN

Build your personal brand

In customer service, how well you honour your commitments shapes how others perceive you. Actions, not words, are your personal brand, so be intentional about the impression you create.

Credibility is built over time through consistent actions and positive customer interactions. It establishes you as a trustworthy and knowledgeable professional who provides exceptional service.

Start by identifying your unique qualities, strengths, values and passions. What sets you apart from others? What do you want to be known for? Be authentically you.

Go above and beyond to meet customer needs and expectations. Your reputation as a reliable, caring, helpful and empathetic service provider is the foundation of your brand.

'*Stop managing your time. Start managing your focus.*'

ROBIN SHARMA

Seize your day

Demands can be unpredictable in customer service, so effective time management is crucial.

Start by identifying and prioritising daily tasks based on urgency and importance.

Set and write down daily, weekly and monthly goals.

While you cannot always predict workflow, this helps you stay focused on what must be accomplished. Allocate time blocks for different types of tasks, such as responding to emails, handling calls and working on projects. Wherever possible, stick to these blocks to minimise distractions.

Focus on one task at a time to improve productivity and reduce errors. Multi-tasking is a myth that only leads to inefficiency.

Limit interruptions by silencing non-essential notifications, closing unnecessary browser tabs or applications, and, where possible, setting clear boundaries for when you are available to colleagues or customers.

Take scheduled breaks to refresh your mind and improve your focus.

'The human desire to be taken
care of never goes away.'

Will Guidara

Provide exceptional service in a fast-paced environment

Delivering world-class service in a fast-paced environment requires balancing efficiency and exceptional customer care.

Despite the busyness, never rush customer interactions. Acknowledge each customer with a smile and eye contact to let them know you have seen them – particularly if there is a queue.

Thank those who have been waiting for their patience.

'Commit yourself to lifelong learning. The most valuable asset you'll ever have is your mind and what you put into it.'

Brian Tracy

Be a lifelong learner

Enhance your world-class customer service skills by continuously seeking improvement, acting upon feedback and committing to life-long learning.

Stay updated with industry trends, customer service best practices, and new technologies that can enhance your performance. Expand your knowledge through reading, audiobooks and podcasts.

Embrace a beginner's mindset, which means approaching things as though you are encountering them for the first time.

Keep an open mind and actively seek constructive feedback from customers and leaders. Be proactive. Analyse and address any identified areas for improvement in your customer service skills.

Part Two

World-Class
Communication Skills

'Listening is a master skill for personal and professional greatness.'

Robin Sharma

Listen attentively

Active listening is one of the greatest gifts we can give each other. In a world filled with distractions, maintaining focus is an art. True mastery lies in offering undivided attention to those we serve.

In customer service, listening is crucial for accuracy and building rapport; it helps us get things right the first time and reduces unnecessary errors and rework. A useful tip is to take notes while talking to the customer, to get all the information and show that you are taking their enquiry or feedback seriously. Always seek permission to do this first.

Customers feel important and valued when they receive your full attention.

'Language creates reality. Words have power. Speak always to create joy.'

Deepak Chopra

Practise world-class language

In the world of luxury and hospitality, five-star hotels pride themselves on their service and impeccable language, reflecting their professionalism, elegance and warmth.

Guests are greeted with courteous and polished language from the moment they arrive. They are addressed by their titles or last names and with formal salutations. 'Good morning', 'Good afternoon' and 'Welcome' are standard practice.

The language is always positive and affirmative. Instead of saying 'I don't know,' staff are encouraged to respond with 'Let me find out for you' or 'I'll be happy to check on that'. These demonstrate the willingness to go the extra mile. Respond with positive words and phrases such as 'You're welcome'. 'Of course.' 'That is my pleasure.' 'Certainly.' 'Absolutely.'

This language is transferrable to most service environments. The formality of your approach may depend on your industry. Whatever your situation, infusing your conversations with world-class language elevates your conversation and honours your customers.

'What lies in our power to do, it
lies in our power not to do.'

ARISTOTLE

Use inclusive language

Creating an inclusive environment makes customers feel welcomed, included and at ease.

Rather than assuming gender, use gender-neutral language. This is simply done by replacing gendered pronouns with 'they' or 'them.' Instead of saying 'him' or 'her', say 'them'.

Use inclusive greetings and interactions, such as 'Hi everyone', instead of gendered addresses. Use people's names if you know them. Consider displaying pronouns on email signatures, badges and in first time introductions to show you are an ally.

Understanding and respecting the impact of language fosters inclusivity in customer interactions.

'Your body language shapes who you are.'

AMY CUDDY

Speak without words

Your body language can reveal your thoughts and feelings without saying a word. It is one of the most essential aspects of face-to-face communication. Many gestures are unconscious, and we are never entirely accurate at interpreting facial expressions.

To avoid misinterpretations, keep your body language open, positive and neutral to signal that you welcome others into your space and are comfortable in their presence.

Closed gestures, such as crossed arms, create nonverbal barriers. A relaxed and pleasant expression demonstrates interest and attentiveness to the customer. Adjust your facial expression to respond helpfully to the emotions of the person you are dealing with. Smiling when they make a complaint will only annoy them.

'I have a big thing with eye contact

because as soon as you make eye

contact with somebody, you see them,

and they become valued and worthy.'

MARY LAMBERT

Maintain eye contact

Appropriate eye contact signals that you are entirely focused on what the customer is saying. That helps them perceive you as sincere.

Cultural norms regarding eye contact differ significantly. In some cultures, prolonged or direct eye contact shows attentiveness and respect. In others, it may be seen as confrontational or disrespectful.

Make brief eye contact during busy periods to let the customer know you have seen them; this will reduce any anxiety on their part.

*'To effectively communicate, we must
realize that we are all different in
the way we perceive the world, and
use this understanding as a guide to
our communication with others.'*

TONY ROBBINS

Treat people how they want to be treated

All your customers have unique needs, preferences and communication styles. While it is often said that we should treat people as we want to be treated, taking service to the next level requires a shift in thinking. It means treating people how *they* want to be treated.

Communication styles range from direct to indirect; some customers love to chat, while others get straight to the point. These styles are not right or wrong; they're just different.

Adapting your approach to suit the customer allows you to establish rapport and connection and build a strong relationship, regardless of your differences.

'The single biggest problem in communication is the illusion that it has taken place.'

Gᴇᴏʀɢᴇ Bᴇʀɴᴀʀᴅ Sʜᴀᴡ

Communicate clearly

Use clear and concise language when interacting with customers.

Avoid acronyms, technical terms and jargon that people outside your field or industry won't easily understand. Don't assume that they know what you are talking about. Ask questions, listen to their responses and watch their body language to be sure you understand each other.

When customers don't fully get what you're saying, it can lead to mistakes, frustration and even disputes.

'Ask the right questions and the answers will always reveal themselves.'

Oprah Winfrey

Use open questions

Asking 'How may I help you?' instead of 'Can I help you?' can significantly impact customer interactions.

'How' questions are open-ended; they encourage customers to share their needs and preferences freely.

'Can I help you?' is a closed question that may prompt a simple 'No' response and limit your opportunity to understand the customer's requirements.

A slight adjustment in wording can make all the difference.

'In diversity there is beauty
and there is strength.'

MAYA ANGELOU

Embrace cultural intelligence

In our diverse world, effectively interacting and adapting to different cultural contexts is a valuable skill.

Cultural awareness recognises that people are not the same and understands that we hold different values, behaviours and perspectives. Treat all individuals with respect, courtesy and sensitivity while actively acknowledging and showing interest in cultural differences.

Awareness and knowledge are the first steps to understanding. Learn. Educate yourself about different cultures, customs, traditions and social norms.

Approach each person and culture with an open mind, free from preconceived notions and biases. Embrace and respect cultural diversity, even if it differs from your personal beliefs and practices.

Adapt your behaviours and approaches to accommodate cultural differences and show flexibility.

Cultivate a lifelong learning mindset regarding cultural intelligence. Stay curious and open to new experiences. Continually seek opportunities to expand your knowledge and understanding of different cultures.

'Learn continually – there's always
"one more thing" to learn!'

STEVE JOBS

Seek the answer

Whether you are a seasoned professional or new to customer service, you will encounter questions you can't immediately answer.

In such situations, respond confidently and say, 'That's a great question. Let me clarify that for you.'

Saying 'Um, I'm not sure, I don't really know' can undermine the customer's confidence in your abilities.

Take the initiative to find the correct information and promptly get back to the customer.

Incorrect information can have detrimental effects, so deliver accurate details from the outset. Customers don't mind if you don't have the answer as long as you make a concerted effort to find out and get back to them promptly.

Remember that working in customer service involves continual learning.

'If you just communicate, you can
get by. But if you communicate
skillfully, you can work miracles.'

JIM ROHN

Navigate moments of silence

Avoid long silences or 'dead air' during phone conversations with customers.

Use verbal nods like 'Right' and 'Yes' to signal active listening.

Build rapport by asking relevant questions, like, 'Has it been a busy day for you today?'

If you have to pause the conversation, keep the customer informed about your actions, saying, 'I am just bringing up those details for you now.' Or, 'I will now read through your notes so you will hear a minute or so of silence.'

These approaches create engaging and attentive customer service experiences, leaving a positive impression and facilitating effective communication during phone interactions.

'The key to mitigating disloyalty
is reducing customer effort.'

MATTHEW DIXON

Facilitate warm transfers

All telephone interactions should aim for first-call resolution; however, transferring a customer to another person or department may sometimes be necessary.

If you must transfer a call, view it as a positive way to support the customer and yourself.

Remember, great service means the customer does not have to repeat themselves.

Always announce the customer and pass on any details to the relevant party. If you receive a transfer, use whatever details you have to build the customer relationship.

'Time management is a misnomer; the challenge is to manage ourselves.'

STEPHEN R. COVEY

Set a timeframe

Setting a timeframe involves skilfully guiding your customer during interactions. It's especially useful when dealing with talkative customers or during lengthy discussions, as it establishes parameters and facilitates a prompt and courteous conclusion.

To effectively manage the conversation, consider phrases such as: 'I appreciate your time, and I'll be brief' (even if they initiated the call). 'I understand you have a busy schedule, so I'll be concise.' 'Let me cover one final point before we conclude.' 'I want to respect your time, so I won't take much longer.' 'I'll start working on this immediately to move the process along for you.'

Balancing service and efficiency avoids unnecessary delays for other customers. These strategies demonstrate respect for the customer's time while ensuring a satisfactory and efficient resolution.

'We need to remember across generations that there is as much to learn as there is to teach.'

GLORIA STEINEM

Value generational differences

~⁓~

Awareness of generational differences has become crucial in building successful and lasting customer relationships.

Each generation brings unique expectations and communication preferences, requiring a nuanced approach. Tailor your approach to generational inclinations by considering how customers prefer to communicate through social media, live chat or traditional phone support.

Gen Z, for instance, may seek tech-savvy and fast-paced online interactions, while Baby Boomers may appreciate patience and a more personal touch.

That said, watch for stereotypes and cultivate a customer-centric mindset, recognising individual preferences within each generation.

'If there is any chance you think
your email will be misinterpreted,
it will be. Pick up the phone!'

MARSHA EGAN

Craft thoughtful email responses

Emails are an opportunity to foster positive relationships and shape customers' perceptions of you and your organisation.

But before you send an email, consider whether it is the best communication channel for your message. Is it better to deliver the message by phone, in-person or video?

An effective email is one that the recipient can easily understand. It must be free from spelling, grammar and punctuation errors and jargon.

Depending on the purpose and the content, consider using a friendly and conversational tone — as if you were speaking directly to the customer. Be careful, though, as written words can be easily misinterpreted.

Personalise template responses.

Once written, reread the email to ensure all questions are answered. Check for errors and verify details like names, events and dates.

Before hitting send, consider the recipient's emotional response when reading it.

Although it may seem like extra effort, your customers will genuinely appreciate the difference when they receive a well-crafted email in their inbox.

'*Be mindful when it comes to your words. A string of some that don't mean much to you, may stick with someone else for a lifetime.*'

RACHEL WOLCHIN

Emphasise positive language

Words have power. Psychologists say even hearing a negative word like 'No' can set off an alarm in your brain and trigger the release of stress-producing hormones.

How can words make such a difference in the customer's response?

Positive, proactive language demonstrating care and willingness to help can make or break customer service interactions. Customers are more likely to respond positively to a can-do attitude.

Little changes in how you use language can have a major impact.

Focus on delivering positive messages first and telling customers what you can do for them. Replace 'No', 'Can't', 'Don't' and 'Won't' with 'What I can do' and 'What I will do'.

The right words can transform the customer experience. Choose them wisely.

'Building a great customer experience does not happen by accident. It happens by design.'

CLARE MUSCUTT

Keep customers informed

Provide timely updates to build trust and demonstrate your commitment to the customer.

When you proactively share information, you manage their expectations and empower customers to make informed decisions.

Whether you're informing them about the status of their enquiry, explaining the progress of a support request or providing updates on an order or a project, keeping customers in the loop fosters transparency, reduces uncertainty and enhances their overall experience.

'Diligent follow-up and follow-through
will set you apart from the crowd
and communicate excellence.'

JOHN C. MAXWELL

Close the service loop

Closing the loop in customer service involves following up with customers after their issue or enquiry has been resolved.

This proactive step demonstrates your commitment, provides reassurance and can turn a standard interaction into a memorable one.

Reach out to the customer shortly after their request has been resolved, typically within a day or two. Reiterate your availability to help with any further questions or concerns.

While a job, task or request may have been completed, failure to inform the customer means they may not know and even unnecessarily reach out again to check on the status of their request. A brief email or SMS is sometimes all that is needed.

'Raise your words, not your voice. It is
rain that grows flowers, not thunder.'

RUMI

Focus on your tone of voice

Your voice is a powerful tool, as your tone conveys your thoughts and emotions. That means avoiding sounding monotonous and exuding a bright, engaging and positive demeanour when interacting with a customer.

Vary your tone, and remember that a smile carries in your voice. If a customer's tone reflects distress or concern, then show empathy and understanding. Always maintain an interested and friendly tone to communicate your readiness to assist and provide exceptional service.

Part Three

Manage Challenging Situations

'Your unhappiest customers are your greatest source of learning.'

BILL GATES

Welcome feedback

Feedback comes in many forms. Welcome it all.

Thank the customer sincerely for letting you know their feedback, even if it is negative.

Remember, the customer had two choices: to share it with you or tell someone else.

Always end an interaction on a positive note. For example, 'Thank you so much for letting us know. We appreciate you giving us a chance to fix this issue'.

Make sure this is not lip service and there are no barriers to the customers' ability to give feedback.

'As long as you have the courage to admit
mistakes, things can be turned around.'

HARUKI MURAKAMI

Admit mistakes gracefully

If you make a mistake, acknowledge it honestly and make amends promptly.

Customers appreciate honesty, and when you take responsibility for errors, it builds trust.

Remember, nobody is perfect, and even the best businesses make mistakes. What sets them apart is how they handle those mistakes.

When you admit fault, do so with sincerity. Acknowledge the issue, apologise, take ownership and assure the customer that you're committed to resolving it. Use the opportunity to learn and improve and avoid the mistake happening again.

Customers understand that everyone makes mistakes. What they truly value is your willingness to make things right.

'Even if a conversation is difficult,

we must still be loving, gentle,

decent, honest, moral, honorable,

virtuous and full of integrity.'

DELORES JAMES

Help customers get back on track

Whenever you get caught up with a customer who is going off-topic, tactfully steer the conversation back to their main issue. Acknowledge what they have been discussing so they don't feel you are dismissing them.

This strategy can be handy with an overly talkative customer.

For example, if the customer starts talking about a past issue, use a back-on-track technique such as, 'I can certainly hear that would have been extremely difficult for you. Now in relation to ...'

This redirect shows acknowledgement while keeping control of the conversation.

'One of the best lessons you can learn in life is to master how to remain calm.'

Catherine Pulsifer

Manage customers who talk over you

Conversations with customers who talk over or interrupt you can be incredibly frustrating. There are various reasons why they might do so, such as excitement, impatience, lack of active listening or a desire to control the conversation. Different communication styles and a lack of awareness about the impact of interrupting can also contribute to the issue.

Remain calm and composed, and set clear expectations about the need for equal participation and active listening.

Demonstrate empathy and summarise the customer's concerns to redirect the focus of the conversation. Speak confidently and clearly; politely assert that you want to provide the necessary information or address their concerns.

If the customer interrupts, pause and then politely interject. Say, for example, 'I understand your point and would appreciate it if you could allow me to provide some information that might help resolve the issue.' By calmly intervening, you rebalance the conversation.

'Between stimulus and power is our greatest choice, the freedom to choose.'

STEPHEN R. COVEY

Choose your response

In life, there will always be circumstances that are beyond your control or ability to change. However, the thing that is always in your power is your choice of how to respond.

Customers or colleagues who are having a difficult day do not inherently cause you to become angry or negative. That response is always your choice, although it is not always simple.

Embrace and practice this empowering belief every day.

'Patience is never more important than
when you are at the edge of losing it.'

O. A. BATTISTA

Practice patience

Maintain patience and composure in challenging situations. Handling difficulties with grace reflects your professionalism.

When engaging with customers, resist the urge to jump to conclusions or formulate responses prematurely. Instead, give your full attention to what they're saying. Listen to the words and the tone, emotions and underlying concerns.

Empathise with their perspective and make an effort to understand their situation. Repeat key points or paraphrase their concerns to show that you're truly engaged and comprehend their needs. This simple action validates their feelings and gives them confidence.

'Empathy has no script. There is no right way or wrong way to do it. It's simply listening, holding space, withholding judgement, emotionally connecting and communicating that incredibly healing message of "You're not alone".'

BRENÉ BROWN

Support customers through grief and loss

Empathy with grieving customers can provide comfort when we can't alleviate their pain.

Grief is a natural response whose intensity varies with the magnitude of the loss. Acknowledge their loss with a heartfelt expression of sympathy, such as, 'I am deeply sorry for your loss' or 'I can't imagine how difficult this must be for you.'

Grieving customers may display shock, anger, sadness or even numbness; these emotions are a response to their loss, not a reflection on you.

Avoid clichés about death, such as 'They are in a better place.' Resist the urge to share your own story, as it may minimise the customer's experience.

Be patient and allow silence. Sometimes, they might need to pause, cry, or take a moment.

Recognise that some people may have had complicated connections with the deceased. Allow them to express feelings of guilt, anger or sorrow without judgement.

Offering a compassionate ear and a caring heart can truly make a significant difference in times of need.

These conversations can be emotionally taxing, so remember that your role is to be an understanding and empathetic ear – not a grief counsellor. Seek support from a colleague or leader if required.

'An organisation can't please every human being every time. But it never hurts to try.'

Horst Schulze

Accept that you can't please everybody

Working in customer service means you can never give customers what they want every time. You won't always satisfy every customer – no matter how hard you try.

Accepting this is not easy when you are service-oriented.

If you have done everything possible, remind yourself that you have exhausted all avenues.

If the customer is still unhappy, accept that there may be factors beyond your control. You can't please everyone all the time.

'Where focus goes, energy flows.'

TONY ROBBINS

Engage the 90-second rule

The 90-second rule is valuable for managing your emotions after an upsetting or annoying incident.

When something negative occurs, take 90 seconds to acknowledge and experience any anger or frustration you may feel. Then, consciously decide to release those emotions and not dwell on the situation or person any longer, freeing yourself from unnecessary negative thoughts and conserving your energy.

This step is important in customer-facing roles, especially when dealing with challenging interactions, where getting caught up in thoughts about rude or difficult customers is common.

You don't have to excuse the customer's behaviour to recognise the benefit of simply letting go.

There is often minimal time between phone calls, face-to-face encounters or digital communication. Transitioning into the next interaction with a positive mindset can transform your day.

The next time you dwell on a previous interaction, gift yourself 90 seconds to process your feelings and then choose to let them go. You'll discover the remarkable difference it can make.

'Try not to react merely in the moment.
Pull back from the situation. Take a
wider view. Compose yourself.'

EPICTETUS

Manage sarcasm

Sarcasm is derived from the Greek word *sarkázein*, meaning 'to tear flesh'. It can disguise underlying emotions like anger, fear or hurt in cutting or sneering remarks. Sarcasm is less genuine and more hostile than clever wit. When a customer uses sarcasm, it may hide insecurity, anger or social awkwardness.

While sarcasm can be hurtful and passive-aggressive, understand that individual triggers can provoke intense emotional reactions. These could be a tone of voice, specific words or opinions.

When faced with sarcasm from a customer, control your reaction. Pause and breathe to stay calm and in control. Don't respond or engage with sarcasm; focus on the customer's content or issue. If necessary, politely ask the customer to refrain from making sarcastic comments while expressing your willingness to help. If the behaviour becomes unacceptable, follow your organisation's formal escalation policy.

'No one can make you feel inferior

without your consent.'

ELEANOR ROOSEVELT

Avoid taking things personally

'Don't take it personally' is easier said than done. However, there are significant benefits to refusing to feel insulted.

Minimising time spent dwelling on the interaction reduces stress and enables quicker recovery. Reacting to perceived slights can negatively impact future customer interactions, escalating conflicts from heightened stress.

Although challenging, remember that the customer's anger is often directed at the process or outcome, not you. Not taking it personally creates an invisible wall around you, allowing hurtful comments to bounce off. Recognise that they are angry about the situation, and you just happen to be the target.

Distancing yourself from their words is a conscious choice.

'The customer is not always right ... But,
they are always the customer, so let them
be wrong with dignity and respect.'

Shep Hyken

The customer is not always right

'The customer is always right' is a slogan promoting customer satisfaction, popularised by successful retailers Harry Gordon Selfridge, John Wanamaker and Marshall Field.

As early as 1914, this view disregarded dishonest or unrealistic customers. Despite its enduring presence in popular culture, customers are not always right. They can be misinformed or unaware, just like anyone else, but it is not always deliberate.

In challenging conversations, customers may indeed be wrong. Instead of bluntly stating it, use the opportunity to educate or explain without diminishing their self-esteem. Avoid arguing or engaging in a battle of wits. Focus on maintaining a respectful dialogue.

Say 'Are you aware ...' or 'Please allow me to explain ...' to educate the customer while preserving their self-esteem.

*'Of all positive memories customers
have of good service, fully 25% started
as a service-delivery failure.'*

JANELLE BARLOW

Recognise a complaint as a gift

Every time a customer makes a complaint, remember they had options. They could tell you (or the world!) or remain silent and never return.

Embrace every complaint as a valuable gift and an opportunity for improvement. Instead of focusing on how the complaint is delivered, focus on why they are complaining, what can be done to prevent it from happening again and how to repair and rebuild the relationship.

If you receive a complaint, own it. Even if you weren't personally responsible, you are acting on behalf of the organisation. Remember, every complaint is an opportunity to build loyalty.

'Breathe, pause for a moment, breathe, focus on the breath. Know you are ok, in this moment.'

LEO BABAUTA

Fit your own oxygen mask first

During aircraft safety briefings, flight attendants emphasise the importance of putting on your oxygen mask before assisting others.

This rule applies when dealing with upset customers.

Handling intense emotions and complex customer issues is difficult, but remaining calm and controlling your emotional state is crucial.

When faced with a challenging customer, start by managing your reactions. Recognise that your fight-flight-freeze response is activated when you feel threatened or stressed.

To regain control, practice breathing in for four counts and exhale for four counts. Slow down and focus your thoughts. This technique helps you respond appropriately to the situation.

'Don't think or judge, just listen.'

Sarah Dessen

Let customers share their stories

Allow upset customers to express themselves without interruption. Listen attentively and wait until they've finished speaking before responding or taking any action.

Maintain your composure and keep personal feelings aside. Look at the situation objectively and understand that the customer's anger is often directed towards what happened – not you personally.

Remember, the customer won't be receptive to resolving the situation until they've fully expressed their emotions.

'Empathy is seeing with the eyes of another, listening with the ears of another and feeling with the heart of another.'

Alfred Adler

Acknowledge customers' emotions

Empathy is the key to handling complex customer interactions.

When you acknowledge and empathise with the customer's emotions, you show that you understand their perspective. That helps them focus their frustration on the issue rather than directing it at you.

Utilise sincere empathy statements and tailor your response to their specific situation. Use phrases such as 'I can hear ...'. 'I can appreciate ...'. 'I can understand ...'.

Building rapport through empathy allows you to approach the problem from the customer's point of view, fostering a more constructive resolution.

'A truly humble apology works to part
storm clouds, calm rough seas, and
bring on the soft lights of dawn; it has
the power to change a person's world.'

RICHELLE E. GOODRICH

Offer an apology

Apologising is another way of connecting with the customer. Offering a sincere apology does not admit blame; it establishes rapport.

It doesn't matter who or what was at fault. It is an acknowledgement that things are not going right, even if you weren't personally responsible.

Keep apologies sincere, personal and neutral, and use 'I' instead of 'We'. For example, 'I am sorry that you have been kept waiting', or 'I am sorry this has been your experience.' Make apologies timely, too – the sooner, the better.

'Responsibility equals accountability equals ownership. And a sense of ownership is the most powerful weapon a team or organisation can have.'

PAT SUMMITT

Take ownership of the issue

Your ability to respond and resolve a customer's issue is critical. Some things can be resolved on the spot. Speed is always preferable, as quicker action often gives a better outcome and experience.

You may have to investigate further if it can't be resolved immediately. Commit to getting back to the customer promptly and deliver on your promise.

If you can, give the customer a specific timeframe; this sets a realistic expectation and avoids them needing to call back to check on progress.

'Bad news isn't wine. It doesn't improve with age.'

COLIN POWELL

Deliver bad news gently

Sometimes, you may have to tell a customer news they don't want to hear – or an outcome that is not in their favour.

Don't delay. Just like removing a band-aid, it's better to get it over quickly. Procrastination only worsens the customer's reaction.

If any options are available, present these first. If absolutely nothing can be done, explain the reason behind the situation. Education and information play a vital role.

Conclude the conversation with empathy. Showing genuine concern and care for the customer may be as simple as saying, 'I wish there were something further I could do'.

'Customers don't expect you to be perfect. They do expect you to fix things when they go wrong.'

DONALD PORTER

Instigate swift service recovery

There's a significant opportunity for service recovery once a complaint is successfully resolved.

Simply rectifying an issue that should never have occurred in the first place may not fully restore the customer's confidence. Consider what other measures might be available. These might involve offering a gift, sending a handwritten card, following up with an email, or making a personal phone call.

Demonstrating genuine care through a meaningful and thoughtful gesture can significantly rebuild the customer's trust and faith in you.

'All human behavior has a reason.

All behavior is solving a problem.'

Michael Crichton

All behaviour has meaning

When things go wrong for a customer, they may be emotional or irrational.

Become like Sherlock Holmes looking through a magnifying glass. Stay focused on the issue and avoid getting caught up in their problems.

Focus on the issue, not the behaviour.

'Negative energy is always fishing for more negativity. You have a choice not to take the bait.'

DOREEN VIRTUE

Don't take the bait

In difficult situations, disgruntled customers may bait you to provoke a reaction.

They may employ verbal and non-verbal behaviours to get you to react, giving them control of the conversation.

This tactic can leave you off-balance and angry as customers make comments or insults such as 'I pay your wages' to claim authority or blame you.

In response, you have two choices: take the bait and react, or ignore it and rephrase their comments positively. The latter option defuses the situation, saves time and energy and promotes rational and positive communication.

'We do not learn from experience, we learn from reflecting on experience.'

JOHN DEWEY

Engage in personal debriefing

Debriefing may be important after a difficult conversation, yet it cannot always happen immediately. Personal reflection is valuable. Ask yourself three questions.

1. What did I do well?
2. What would I do differently next time?
3. Do I need any additional help or support from my leader?

Every conversation is a learning opportunity; this technique will improve self-awareness and future interactions.

*'There is a difference between giving
up and strategic disengagement.
Know the difference.'*

Bryant McGill

Disengage respectfully

If a customer is going around in circles and the conversation appears to be going nowhere, it may be time to disengage politely.

You need to find the balance between efficiency and your ability to serve other customers or take the next call.

Use polite and assertive language such as, 'As there is nothing further I can add to this conversation, I will have to leave this here'.

Thank the customer for their time.

'Most people do not listen with the intent to understand; they listen with the intent to reply.'

STEPHEN R. COVEY

Manage customers who won't listen

Dealing with customers who don't listen can be extremely challenging and requires much patience.

When customers don't listen, they may genuinely not understand. They might say, 'You're not making any sense'. Or they may not want to understand when you deliver an unfavourable outcome or disappointing information.

Your job is to remain calm and in control. Don't interrupt or talk over them.

Politely interject, if required, for example, 'Sorry to interrupt you [name], may I ask some clarifying questions so I can assist you?'.

Avoid expressions such as 'You are not listening to me' as this will only escalate the situation. Continue to repeat your message until they have understood. Rephrase your message with different words or expressions. Perhaps offer to put your message in writing.

Acknowledge and empathise if the customer is unhappy with the outcome, for example, 'I am sorry we cannot meet your request'.

If they still don't listen, restate your position and bring the conversation to a close. Maintain confidence and assertiveness throughout the interaction.

'Discretion is a synonym for intelligence.'

ELOISA JAMES

170

Exercise discretion

Think carefully about what you share with a customer. While explanations can be beneficial, certain things should be kept within the organisation.

Avoid airing dirty laundry or laying interdepartmental blame. Criticising another person or department within your organisation contributes to negative customer perception.

'An upset customer is understandable;

an abusive customer is unacceptable.'

RON KAUFMAN

Establish clear boundaries

Nobody in customer service is paid to be abused. There is a clear distinction between an angry or upset customer and an abusive one. Everyone deserves to feel safe at work.

If a customer uses abusive language, threats or discrimination, it's time to set boundaries. Politely address the issue by acknowledging their frustration and requesting them to refrain from using such language or comments.

Inform them that the conversation will be terminated if the behaviour persists.

If it continues further, disconnect the conversation, inform your leader and file a report.

Remember, our purpose is to help customers, not endure abuse.

Part Four

Self-care and Resilience

'*Stay away from negative people. They have a problem for every solution.*'

ALBERT EINSTEIN

Avoid negativity

Some people have to blow out the candles to see how dark it is. They are constantly negative and find fault with anything and everyone.

While you might empathise, you can choose not to join in the negativity.

Redirect the conversation by asking, 'So what do you think may help?'

If necessary, walk away.

Protect your energy at all costs.

*'It's not what you do – it's what you
do in-between what you do – that
really matters! The Third Space is that
moment of transition between one
role or task to the next role or task.'*

ADAM FRASER

Reset between service interactions

The ability to reset between interactions is essential in high-contact customer environments. Pause and take a few deep breaths. This simple practice can help you relax and clear your mind.

The trick is to avoid carrying any negative emotions or frustrations from one interaction to the next. Focus on the customer at hand.

Sip water to stay hydrated and refresh your mind. Dehydration can negatively affect concentration.

Physical movement can also help by releasing tension and boosting your energy levels.

Visualise a positive outcome for the upcoming interaction.

'Rest and self-care are so important.
When you take time to replenish
your spirit, it allows you to serve
others from the overflow. You cannot
serve from an empty vessel.'

ELEANOR BROWN

Prioritise self-care

—⁓—

Self-care is crucial when taking care of customers. Every day, focus on three key areas:

Health and wellbeing: Get enough sleep, exercise regularly and stay hydrated.

Daily habits: Take breaks and stretch if sitting for long periods. Practice daily gratitude and mindfulness. Manage your digital consumption and make time for hobbies.

Connection: Foster team connections and ask for help when needed. Maintain relationships with supportive individuals (friends, family, colleagues, pets).

Remember to prioritise self-care every day.

'Almost everything will work
again if you unplug it for a few
minutes, including you.'

ANNE LAMOTT

Take your breaks

Physical and mental breaks maintain a sense of freshness and focus when engaging with customers. No matter how busy your day may be, allocate time for breaks.

Whether it is a brief respite or a designated break, make it a habit to step away from your desk.

Take a walk outside during your lunch break, or change your surroundings.

We all need time to rest and recuperate, as it improves levels of concentration and focus. It is particularly important when working from home. Planned breaks throughout the day give you time to switch off and refocus.

Self-care nurtures your wellbeing. It is an investment in you and the quality of your interactions.

'I have so much to accomplish today that I must meditate for two hours instead of one.'

MAHATMA GANDHI

Create a daily meditation practice

Meditation is a mind-body practice of staying present with your breath for a specific period to promote awareness and cultivate wellbeing.

There are numerous documented mental and physical health benefits from meditation. These include reducing stress, lowering blood pressure, strengthening the immune system, improving memory, concentration and focus and improving sleep and overall mood.

Start with a morning or evening meditation practice (or both). Try apps like Headspace, Calm or Smiling Mind.

'Deep human connection is ... the purpose and the result of a meaningful life – and it will inspire the most amazing acts of love, generosity, and humanity.'

MELINDA GATES

Schedule time for connection

Humans are wired for connection. We all have different preferences; some are extroverted and energised by being with people, while others are introverted and prefer to recharge with time alone.

Whatever your preference, making time for connection is essential.

In the busyness of life, weeks and months fly by before we know it. Connecting with family and friends and spending time with pets and others who bring us joy is enormously valuable. That might be scheduling a monthly date night with your partner or best friend, organising the annual family get-together or holiday, or simply walking the dog every day.

Connection is far more likely to happen if it is in your diary. We all need connection and time with those who revitalise us. Schedule it and make it happen.

*'Sleep is the investment in the energy
you need to be effective tomorrow.'*

Tom Rath

Invest in sleep

—∽—

While we all need varying amounts of sleep, adequate rest is essential for good health. The quantity and quality of sleep you get each night impacts your immune system and your mood.

Wherever possible, establish a sleep schedule with a regular wakeup time, winding down to prepare for bed and a regular time to sleep. Your circadian rhythm, the physiological procedure your body uses to control your sleep and waking cycle, depends on it.

Try putting your phone, tablet, alarm clock and other devices across the room or (better still) outside your room to prevent distractions or being disturbed in the middle of the night. Set an alarm to remind you of your scheduled bedtime. Finally, have a period away from screens before bedtime to improve your chances of a good night's sleep.

'The key is not to prioritize what's on your schedule, but to schedule your priorities.'

Stephen R. Covey

Create an exercise routine

Exercise is the foundation of good mental and physical health. The challenge can be making it happen in your weekly schedule. The key is to plan it into your day or week and choose to do something you love.

For some, that may be going to the gym, while for others, it could be walking, dancing, yoga or Pilates. Or catching up with friends for a walk and talk.

Use your lunch break to exercise if you have a full diary and competing priorities.

'*Self-care is giving the world the best of you, instead of what's left of you.*'

KATIE REED

Stay hydrated

We cannot survive without water. It is essential for numerous bodily processes, including supplying nutrition to cells, eliminating waste, safeguarding joints and organs and regulating body temperature. It is also crucial for your voice.

Keep a bottle of water beside your desk or use an app to remind you to drink regularly throughout the day.

'Manage your energy, not your time.'

RACHEL WOLCHIN

Conduct an energy audit

Focus on managing your energy rather than your time.

Draw two columns on a piece of paper. At the top of one column, write 'Gives me energy' and on the other, 'Zaps my energy'.

List everything that gives you energy – at work and elsewhere. Commit to doing more of that.

List everything that zaps your energy – at work and elsewhere. Do whatever you can to eliminate or reduce those things.

This activity is worth doing regularly, especially when you feel low on energy.

'I bend so I don't break.'

UNKNOWN

Take stretch breaks every hour

With more time spent at our desks, on Zoom or in virtual meetings, some days feel like we are stuck to our chairs.

Use a standing desk or a fit ball, or stand up and stretch every sixty minutes to avoid getting stiff.

Mobile headsets are useful for walking and talking. Schedule walking meetings. Use the reminder on your phone, watch or app to stand up and move.

*'My day begins and ends
with gratitude and joy.'*

LOUISE HAY

Practice daily gratitude

Gratitude is acknowledging others for their kindness or the positive aspects of our existence. There are numerous documented advantages to regularly practising and expressing gratitude.

Evidence supports that an intentional focus on daily gratitude improves mental health. According to studies, people with a propensity for gratitude exhibit higher levels of brain activity in the medial prefrontal cortex, which is connected to learning and judgement.

In one study, this brain activity was present a month after the test, indicating that the impact of appreciation lingers. Start and end the day with gratitude. Mentally note, or write down, three things you are grateful for.

'We need to be intentional about how, where and when to use our devices. Creating cues, rituals and habits to encourage healthy digital behaviours is vital.'

KRISTY GOODWIN

Monitor your daily digital consumption

—⁓—

Devices can be a source of connection with family and friends but can also lead to endless scrolling and wasted time. Focusing on comparisons or reading news stories of constant negativity causes havoc.

Healthy boundaries with social media and awareness of what you consume are essential for good mental health.

'Passion is energy. Feel the power that comes from focusing on what excites you.'

OPRAH WINFREY

Make time for hobbies and interests

What do you love doing outside of work? What brings you joy and lights you up?

With the demands of working in customer service and life generally, finding time for hobbies and interests can be difficult.

Schedule time for your hobbies at the start of the week or month to ensure it is a priority. Fill your cup with activities that inspire you.

*'When you're working towards a
goal, things get boring, tough, hard,
monotonous, you want to give up, and
what makes you stay the course is
coming back to your reason why.'*

TURIA PITT

Maintain motivation

Some days are tough. You may be asked the same question five times, have a string of difficult interactions or an endless pile of work.

Find purpose in your role by understanding your impact on customers' lives. Recognise that your service makes a meaningful difference.

Celebrate small wins. Acknowledge and reward yourself for successfully handling challenging interactions or achieving your goals.

Keep learning. Acquire new skills and knowledge to make your role more interesting and inspire even better service.

Set goals for the future. Perhaps you want a leadership role or to work in a different department. Engage great mentors and realise anything is possible with drive, determination and hard work.

Seek peer support. No one knows your world as well as they do. Share experiences, advice and coping strategies. Building a supportive network can help you navigate tough situations and sustain motivation.

Prioritise your wellbeing, work-life balance, exercise and relaxation. A healthy lifestyle and reduced stress levels are essential for long-term motivation and job satisfaction in customer service.

Remember that your motivation positively impacts you and the customers you serve.

'Celebrate your success and find humor in your failures. Don't take yourself so seriously. Loosen up and everyone around you will loosen up. Have fun and always show enthusiasm. When all else fails, put on a costume and sing a silly song.'

SAM WALTON

Celebrate successes

Recognise and celebrate successes, both big and small. Positive reinforcement can help to boost morale and motivation.

Keep a 'warm fuzzies' file of customer compliments to reflect on during the tough days.

Tick off the goals you achieve each day.

Celebrate team and organisational successes.

Share compliments and positive customer stories.

Find ways every week to intentionally share individual and collective successes.

'If you're going to live, leave a legacy. Make a mark on the world that can't be erased.'

MAYA ANGELOU

Cultivate your service legacy

In the busyness of taking care of customers, tasks and demands, it is sometimes easy to forget the impact of your work. Customer service makes a difference in people's lives.

Fast forward to five, ten, twenty or even thirty years from now. What mark did you leave on the people you encountered? It's worth remembering that we leave an indelible legacy, regardless of our eventual destinations.

You may work for one company or many. Perhaps you have your own business or will build it in the future. Regardless of the company or the industry you work in, never forget how important you are and the difference you make in the lives of others.

'I don't know what your destiny will
be, but one thing I know: the only
ones among you who will be really
happy are those who will have
sought and found how to serve.'

ALBERT SCHWEITZER

Acknowledgements

I have been surrounded by the most extraordinary support with each book I have written. Firstly, to my amazing husband Scott. My eternal cheerleader and encourager, who continues to support my ideas and every book I want to write. You have been instrumental in ensuring I have space to write and create. Thank you for your daily reminders to keep going and reminding me that anything is possible.

To our beautiful children, Molly, Jai, Kobi and Lucy. It is my greatest joy and honour to be your Mum. I see service in each of your precious souls, and your never-ending support means the absolute world to me. As I now witness our two eldest children working in customer service, I relish their stories and excitement when they make someone's day.

To my beautiful Mum, Marea. She suggested that I write this book, and she reads every one of my newsletters. Each Wednesday, I open my email, knowing there will be an encouraging message about my newsletter from Mum. Thank you for loving and supporting me every day of my life.

To Matt Church. My eternal gratitude for being my greatest teacher and helping me create the vision for my book series. To the entire Thought Leaders Business School Community, for being a place where excellence is the norm.

I could have never envisaged publishing my third book before joining Thought Leaders.

Heartfelt thanks go to Asher Nowlan, Nereda Watson, Sean Tape and Virginia Morris for agreeing to be advance readers of this book. I am so grateful to have you all in my world and I deeply value your heart, expertise, care and passion for the customer and employee experience.

To my wonderful editor, Jenny Magee – what a joy to work with you on my third book. Your patience, wisdom and sage advice continue to inspire me.

To my wonderful Business Manager, Deb Bennett-Oxnam. Thank you for the incredible difference you have made in my life and practice and for all you do to live and breathe world-class service in everything you do.

My thanks to Sylvie Blair from BookPOD for your support in publishing my third book. Your responsiveness and exceptional service are deeply valued.

Sometimes, we feel alone in our journey. I invite you to connect with me on LinkedIn and reach out to me at hello@moniquerichardson.com.au with any questions or if I may be of service to you, your team or your organisation.

You are also welcome to join my community. Please scan the QR code to join my weekly service insights newsletter.

Finally, and most importantly, I wish to acknowledge and honour our customer service community across the globe. You continue to inspire me in many ways, and I am privileged to work with you. The lives you impact, the memories you help to create, and your wisdom continue to inspire me in everything I do.

About the Author

Monique Richardson is a leading international expert in service leadership and customer service whose goal is to help transform customer service cultures through a service leadership-driven approach. Creating a truly customer-focused culture is about putting people first and focusing on the employee experience to ensure a highly engaged and empowered workforce and provide the best customer experiences possible.

Over two decades as a keynote speaker and trainer, Monique has delivered workshops to more than 50,000 people. Monique is the author of *They Serve Like We Lead: How to take care of your people so they take care of your customers* and *Managing Difficult Customer Behaviour: A practical guide for confident conversations*. She offers workshops and regularly speaks at conferences across the globe. Her thoughts have been featured on Sky News, Sunrise, CEO World, The CEO Institute and Business Essentials Daily.

Monique's amazing clients are varied; she has designed and delivered programs for many ASX top 200 companies and works extensively with commercial, government and not-for-profit clients. She partners with organisations to design and deliver bespoke training programs in service transformation, service leadership, service excellence and service recovery.

As a conference speaker, Monique brings experience, passion, excitement and humour to the stage. If you are organising a conference and are looking for a speaker to engage and inspire your audience to take action, contact Monique at hello@moniquerichardson.com.au

Monique is a proud wife and mother of four children (and one fur baby) and lives in Melbourne, Victoria. She is passionate about creating a more caring world, fundraising through her 'Love, Hope and Daisies' foundation, fine dining and always having fun.

hello@moniquerichardson.com.au

+61 402 113 912

www.moniquerichardson.com.au

Love, Hope and Daisies Foundation

The Love, Hope and Daisies Foundation was established in loving memory of my beautiful younger sister Simone, who passed away in 1999, aged 21. Simone's life, although far too brief, had a significant impact. She made a huge difference in so many people's lives through her love and care for everyone she came into contact with.

The foundation is all about making a difference wherever there is a need – through financial donations, fundraising efforts or gifts of time. I am a proud supporter of St Mary's House of Welcome, which provides services to people who are homeless and experiencing poverty, severe and persistent mental health issues and those who are socially marginalised. Five per cent of all profits from my business are donated directly to St Mary's House of Welcome, and we involve friends, family and the community in various fundraising efforts.

The foundation symbol is how Simone used to sign off each letter she wrote to her friends and family. Ten per cent of all profits from the sale of this book will be donated directly to St Mary's House of Welcome. Learn more about them at www.smhow.org.au.

Love, hope and daisies FOUNDATION

Recommended Reading

This is a list of my favourite books about world-class service, communication, managing challenging situations, resilience and self-care. I hope you'll read each of them and be inspired to take action.

Excellence Wins by Horst Schulze

Unreasonable Hospitality by Will Guidara

Raving Fans! by Ken Blanchard

Atomic Habits by James Clear

The Third Space by Adam Fraser

Learned Optimism by Martin Seligman

The 7 Habits of Highly Effective People by Stephen R. Covey

Up Yours!: The Benefits of Radical Self-Care by Mark Butler

Dear Digital, We Need To Talk by Kristy Goodwin

Managing Difficult Customer Behaviour by Monique Richardson